Delaware

by Patricia K. Kummer
Capstone Press
Geography Department

Consultant:
Dr. Barbara E. Benson
Executive Director
Historical Society of Delaware

CAPSTONE
HIGH/LOW BOOKS
an imprint of Capstone Press
Mankato, Minnesota

Capstone High/Low Books are published by Capstone Press
818 North Willow Street, Mankato, Minnesota 56001
http://www.capstone-press.com

Library of Congress Cataloging-in-Publication Data
Kummer, Patricia K.
    Delaware/by Patricia K. Kummer (Capstone Press Geography Department).
    p. cm.—(One nation)
    Includes bibliographical references (p. 45) and index.
    Summary: Gives an overview of the state of Delaware, including its history,
geography, people, and living conditions.
    ISBN 0-7368-0116-2
    1. Delaware—Juvenile literature. [1. Delaware.] I. Capstone Press.
Geography Dept. II. Title. III. Series.
F164.3.K86 1999
975.1—dc21   98-43356
                                                     CIP
                                                     AC

Editorial Credits

Angela Kaelberer, editor; Timothy Halldin, cover designer; Abby Bradford
    and Linda Clavel, illustrators; Sheri Gosewisch and Kimberly Danger,
    photo researchers

Photo Credits

Archive Photos, 22
Cheryl Blair, 5 (bottom), 20
Colephoto/Mark E. Gibson, 10
Delaware Tourism Office, 4 (bottom)
Gerald D. Tang, 14
Henry C. Aldrich, 5 (top)
James P. Rowan, 8, 18
One Mile Up, Inc., 4 (top)
Photophile/Jeff Greenberg, 32
Sally Weigand, cover, 24, 26, 29, 30, 34, 38
Unicorn Stock Photos/Andre Jenny, 6
Uniphoto/Phil Cantor, 16

Table of Contents

Fast Facts about Delaware

State flag

Location: In the mid-Atlantic region of the eastern United States

Size: 2,489 square miles (6,447 square kilometers)

Population: 731,581 (U.S. Census Bureau, 1997 estimate)

Capital: Dover

Date admitted to the Union: December 7, 1787; the first state

Blue hen chicken

Peach blossom

Largest cities:
Wilmington,
Dover, Newark,
Milford, Seaford,
Elsmere, Smyrna,
New Castle,
Middletown,
Georgetown

Nickname:
The First State
State bird:
Blue hen chicken
State flower:
Peach blossom
State tree:
American holly
State song:
"Our Delaware," by
George Hynson
and Will M. S. Brown

American holly

Chapter 1
The du Ponts

Wilmington, Delaware, is known as the "Chemical Capital of the World." The town has many chemical factories. The du Pont family built the first of these factories in Delaware.

In 1800, Éleuthère Irénée du Pont de Nemours (E. I. du Pont) arrived in the United States. He had worked as a chemist in France. Chemists study and work with chemicals. In 1802, du Pont began building gunpowder mills. Gunpowder is a mixture of chemicals. It is used in cannons and guns. The first of du Pont's mills was on Brandywine Creek outside of Wilmington.

Near the mill, du Pont built a village for his workers and their families. In 1803, du Pont built

Exhibits at the Hagley Museum display the history of the du Pont family.

Members of the du Pont family lived at Eleutherian Mills from 1803 until 1958.

a home for his family near the mill. He called his home Eleutherian Mills. Members of the du Pont family lived in this home until 1958.

In 1813, E. I. du Pont bought the Hagley estate. This land was downstream from Eleutherian Mills. Du Pont built more mills on this land. The area became known as the Hagley Yards.

The Hagley Museum
Today, Eleutherian Mills, the village, and the gunpowder mills make up the Hagley Museum.

This outdoor museum is spread over 235 acres (95 hectares) in northwestern Wilmington. Visitors can tour the early du Pont mills, Eleutherian Mills, and restored village buildings.

The Du Pont Company and Family

E. I. du Pont's mills were the beginning of the Du Pont Company. This company is one of the world's largest chemical manufacturers.

The du Pont family became wealthy from their company. Family members used some of their money to build schools and roads in Delaware. Others gave money to Delaware's cities and towns.

T. Coleman du Pont was a great-grandson of E. I. du Pont. Between 1911 and 1924, he built Du Pont Boulevard. Today, Du Pont Boulevard is U.S. Highway 13.

Pierre S. du Pont was another great-grandson of E. I. du Pont. Between 1914 and 1920, he gave $1 million to the University of Delaware at Newark. Between 1920 and 1935, he spent about $6 million building public schools in Delaware.

The du Ponts still use some of their wealth to help others. Each year, the company gives more than $300 million to local communities.

Chapter 2
The Land

Delaware is a mid-Atlantic state. It lies along the middle of the U.S. Atlantic Coast. The Atlantic Ocean forms Delaware's southeastern border.

Three states border Delaware. Pennsylvania is Delaware's northern neighbor. The Delaware River and Delaware Bay form Delaware's eastern border with New Jersey. Maryland borders Delaware to the west and to the south.

Delaware is on the Delmarva Peninsula. A peninsula is a piece of land that is surrounded by water on three sides. One side of a peninsula is connected to land. Parts of Maryland and Virginia share the Delmarva

Delaware has many beaches along the Atlantic Ocean.

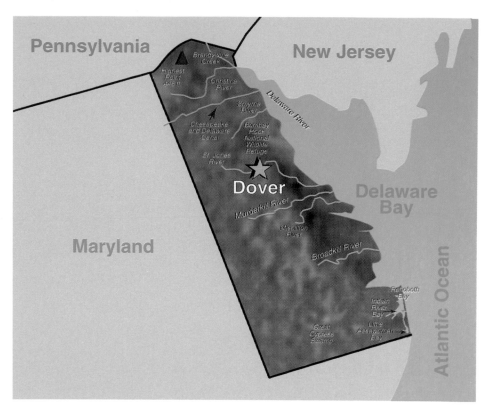

Peninsula with Delaware. The peninsula is named after these three states.

Rivers and Bays

Delaware has several major rivers. The Christina and Smyrna Rivers run through northern Delaware. They empty into the Delaware River. The Delaware River is the state's largest river. It is 280 miles (451 kilometers) long. It flows along northeastern Delaware and empties into Delaware Bay.

Delaware Bay lies between the Delaware River and the Atlantic Ocean. The St. Jones, Murderkill, Mispillion, and Broadkill Rivers flow into Delaware Bay.

Three bays lie along the southeastern Delaware coast. They are Rehoboth, Indian River, and Little Assawoman Bays. Long sandbars separate these bays from the Atlantic Ocean. The ocean's waves formed these ridges of sand. Clams, crabs, and oysters live in these bays.

The Piedmont

The Piedmont covers a small part of northern Delaware. Piedmont means "at the foot of a mountain." Delaware's Piedmont has rolling hills and river valleys. These valleys have rich soil. Brandywine Creek is a major river in the Piedmont.

Delaware's highest point is on the Piedmont. This point is on Ebright Road near Centerville in northern Delaware. The land there rises 448 feet (137 meters) above sea level. Sea level is the average surface level of the world's oceans.

Egrets feed in marshes located on Delaware's Atlantic Coastal Plain.

Atlantic Coastal Plain

The Atlantic Coastal Plain covers the rest of Delaware. The land there is low and flat. The state's lowest point is at sea level on the Atlantic Coastal Plain.

Much of the Atlantic Coastal Plain along Delaware Bay is marshy. Canada geese, egrets, and sandpipers feed in these grassy wetlands. Sandy beaches lie along the Atlantic Ocean.

Farther inland, the Atlantic Coastal Plain has good farmland. Farmers raise potatoes, barley, soybeans, corn, and wheat on this flat land. Dairy cattle graze on the plain's grasses.

Part of the Great Cypress Swamp lies inland on the southern Atlantic Coastal Plain. Some people call this swamp the Great Pocomoke Swamp. Pine, sweet gum, cedar, and cypress trees grow in this 30,000-acre (12,141-hectare) swamp.

Climate

Delaware has a mild climate. Ocean breezes cool the land in the summer. July temperatures average 76 degrees Fahrenheit (24 degrees Celsius). Mountains in Pennsylvania block cold winter winds. January temperatures average 31 degrees Fahrenheit (-1 degree Celsius).

Delaware receives about 39 inches (99 centimeters) of precipitation each year. Precipitation is rain, snow, sleet, or hail. Southeastern Delaware receives the most rain. Northern Delaware receives the most snow.

Chapter 3

The People

Delaware has one of the smallest populations of all U.S. states. Only four states have fewer people. But Delaware's population is growing. Between 1990 and 1997, Delaware's population grew by nearly 10 percent. New jobs brought people from other states to Delaware.

About 75 percent of Delawareans live in or near cities. About 66 percent of Delawareans live in the Wilmington area.

States are divided into areas called counties. Delaware has only three counties. Wilmington is in New Castle County. This county is in the northern part of the state. Kent County is in

About 66 percent of Delaware's people live in the Wilmington area.

Fort Delaware hosts Polish Day each June.

central Delaware. Sussex County covers
southern Delaware.

European Backgrounds

About 76 percent of Delawareans have
European backgrounds. Some can trace their
families back to Delaware's early European
settlers. In the 1600s, people from Sweden,
Britain, and the Netherlands came to what is
now Delaware. Most settled near today's city
of Wilmington.

Other Europeans came to Delaware in the 1800s and early 1900s. In the 1840s, many Irish workers found jobs at the du Pont powder mills. Many Germans opened businesses in Wilmington. Thousands of Italian, Russian, and Polish people arrived in the late 1800s and early 1900s.

Today, many Delawareans honor their European backgrounds. Each March, Irish Americans host a St. Patrick's Day parade in Wilmington. Fort Delaware hosts Polish Day in June. This celebration honors Polish American soldiers who fought in the Civil War (1861–1865).

African Americans

The first African Americans arrived in what is now Delaware in the 1640s. Some were slaves. Others worked as paid servants.

In 1790, about 9,000 slaves lived in Delaware. Most of them worked on plantations. Many of these large farms were in Sussex County.

In 1790, Delaware's government passed a law that made it illegal to bring new slaves into the state. By 1860, about 2,000 slaves and 20,000 free African Americans lived in Delaware.

Many of Delaware's Nanticoke people own truck farms.

Today, African Americans make up about 19 percent of Delaware's population. Many of Delaware's African Americans live in Wilmington. Each July, African Americans celebrate their heritage at Haneef's Annual African Festival and Parade in Wilmington.

Native Americans
About 2,400 Native Americans live in Delaware. They make up about 0.3 percent of the state's population. Most of Delaware's Native

Americans are Nanticoke people. The Nanticoke live throughout Delaware. Some own small businesses. Many Nanticoke are truck farmers. These farmers raise fruits and vegetables to sell at roadside stands.

The Nanticoke tribe owns the Nanticoke Indian Museum in Millsboro. Each September, the Nanticoke hold a powwow there. Native Americans perform traditional songs and dances at powwows. Nanticoke people from all over the United States attend the powwow in Millsboro.

Other Ethnic Groups

Hispanic Americans make up about 3 percent of the state's population. Most of Delaware's Hispanic people came from Puerto Rico. Many Puerto Rican Americans settled in Wilmington. Dover has a large Mexican American population.

Asian Americans make up nearly 2 percent of Delaware's population. Asian Americans are the state's fastest-growing ethnic group. In the 1990s, the number of Asian Americans in Delaware increased by about 35 percent. Most of them came from Taiwan, the Philippines, and South Korea.

Chapter 4
Delaware History

People first arrived in what is now Delaware about 10,000 years ago. By the 1600s, two large Native American groups lived there. They were the Lenape and Nanticoke groups of people. European settlers called the Lenape people the "Delaware." By 1720, most of the Lenape had moved to what is now Ohio. Most of the Nanticoke remained in what is now Delaware.

European Explorers

Explorer Henry Hudson sailed into what is now Delaware Bay in 1609. He was English but worked for the government of the Netherlands. In 1610, other English explorers sailed into the

In 1609, explorer Henry Hudson sailed into what is now Delaware Bay.

The town of Lewes is on the site of the Dutch settlement of Zwaanendael.

bay. They named the bay De La Warr after Thomas West, Lord De La Warr. West was the governor of the Virginia colony. This name later became Delaware.

In 1631, 32 Dutch traders settled near Delaware Bay. These were people from the Netherlands. They called their settlement Zwaanendael (ZWAHN-uhn-dayl). Today, the town of Lewes is on the Zwaanendael site.

Swedish, Dutch, and English Claims
In 1638, Swedish and Finnish settlers founded the colony of New Sweden. They built Fort

Christina in what is now Wilmington. This was the first permanent European settlement in what is now Delaware.

In 1655, the Dutch captured New Sweden. They added it to their land in New York and New Jersey. The Dutch colony was called New Netherland. Great Britain had colonies north and south of New Netherland. In 1664, British forces captured the Dutch lands. At first, what is now Delaware was part of Britain's New York colony. In 1673, the Dutch recaptured these lands. The English regained the lands in 1674.

A New Colony and a Revolution

From 1682 to 1704, what is now Delaware was part of Great Britain's Pennsylvania colony. People called what is now Delaware the "Three Lower Counties on the Delaware." In 1704, Delaware broke away from Pennsylvania. It became the Delaware colony.

In the 1770s, Britain's government placed heavy taxes on goods shipped to the colonies. This led to the Revolutionary War (1775–1783). The colonies became the United States of America after the war ended in 1783.

The Hagley Mills made gunpowder in the early 1800s.

The First State and Early Growth

The United States needed a strong government after the Revolutionary War. In 1787, leaders of the new nation wrote the U.S. Constitution. This document contains the principles for government in the United States.

On December 7, 1787, Delaware approved the Constitution. It was the first state to do so. Delaware's nickname became "The First State."

In the early 1800s, thousands of Europeans found jobs in Delaware. Delaware's textile mills made woolen and cotton cloth. Gunpowder and paper became important Delaware products. Shipping and shipbuilding increased in the state.

Slavery, Civil War, and Growth

By the 1850s, the issue of slavery divided the United States. The Northern states did not allow slavery. Delaware and other Southern states did. Of these states, Delaware had the smallest number of slaves and slaveholders. About 2,000 slaves lived in the state in 1860.

In 1860 and 1861, 11 Southern states left the United States. They formed the Confederate States of America. This led to the Civil War. Delaware's leaders decided to stay in the United States. About 12,000 Delawareans fought for the United States. Almost half of the U.S. Army's gunpowder came from the du Pont mills. In April 1865, the Confederate Army surrendered. In December 1865, slavery was outlawed in the entire United States.

After the war, Delawareans started new businesses and planted new crops. Wilmington factories produced railroad cars and steamships. Delaware's farmers grew many fruits and vegetables. Railroads carried these crops to other eastern states.

World Wars and Depression

In 1917, the United States entered World War I (1914–1918). About 9,000 Delawareans served in the military. Others built ships for the navy or made gunpowder.

Many people in the United States faced financial problems during the Great Depression (1929–1939). Banks and factories closed. Thousands of Delawareans lost their jobs. To help, the United States government started the New Deal in 1933. New Deal programs provided jobs. For example, some Delawareans built picnic areas in the state's forests.

In 1941, the United States entered World War II (1939–1945). Delawareans built ships for the navy. The Du Pont Company made nylon. This new material was used to make parachutes. About 34,000 Delawareans served in the military.

Challenges and Changes

In the late 1800s, Delaware and other Southern states had passed segregation laws. These laws kept people of different races apart in schools and other public places. In 1950, Delaware started integrating its schools to include people of all races. That year, African American students

By the late 1990s, the Delaware River was cleaner than it had been in 100 years.

attended the University of Delaware. The state slowly integrated the rest of its public schools.

Through the 1900s, Delaware's factories brought jobs and money to the state. But waste from many of these factories polluted the Delaware River. In 1971, Delaware's legislature passed the Coastal Zone Act. This act prevents companies from building factories near the Delaware River. The act also protects Delaware Bay and the Atlantic Ocean. By the late 1990s, the Delaware River was cleaner than it had been in 100 years.

Chapter 5
Delaware Business

Manufacturing is Delaware's largest single business. Service businesses are Delaware's largest combined business. Service businesses include banking, government, and trade.

The Corporate State
People sometimes call Delaware the "Corporate State." In 1899, Delaware's legislature passed the General Incorporation Law. This law makes it easy to form a corporation in the state. About 250,000 companies have formed corporations in Delaware. Most of these companies have factories and offices in other states. But they pay taxes to the state of Delaware. This tax money helps the state pay for roads and schools.

More than 40 banks have headquarters in Delaware.

Watermelons are an important Delaware crop.

Manufacturing

Chemicals are Delaware's main manufactured product. The Du Pont Company is Delaware's largest manufacturer. About 12,400 of the state's people work for Du Pont.

Many Delaware factories produce other products. Workers at some Delaware factories package chicken, fish, or baked goods. Others build cars at Chrysler and General Motors plants.

Service Businesses

Government is Delaware's largest employer. About 27,300 Delawareans work in local, state, or federal government jobs.

Delaware's fastest-growing businesses are in finance. These businesses include banks, real estate, and insurance. In the 1980s, Delaware's government lowered taxes on banks. Since then, more than 40 banks from other states have moved to Delaware.

The port of Wilmington is a trading center. This port receives the world's largest shipments of bananas. Ships from Wilmington bring automobiles to ports throughout the world.

Farming and Fishing

Most of Delaware's farms are located in Sussex County. Soybeans are Delaware's leading crop. Potatoes, corn, wheat, watermelons, and alfalfa hay are other important crops.

Other farmers raise livestock. Broiler chickens are Delaware's most valuable farm product. These young chickens are raised for their meat.

Fishing also is important in Delaware. Crabs are Delaware's leading seafood catch. Most of these crabs come from Delaware Bay.

Chapter 6

Seeing the Sights

Visitors to Delaware can enjoy many activities throughout the year. Many people enjoy the outdoors at Delaware's beaches and state parks. Others learn about the state's history at its museums and historic homes.

Around Wilmington

In 1638, European settlers sailed to what is now Wilmington on the Swedish warship *Kalmar Nyckel*. Today, visitors can see a copy of this ship in Wilmington. The ship is 105 feet (32 meters) tall and more than 97 feet (30 meters) long. Visitors also can learn about the Swedish settlers at the Kalmar Nyckel Shipyard and Museum.

A copy of the *Kalmar Nyckel* ship is in Wilmington.

Old Swedes Church is near the museum. Swedish settlers built this church in 1698. It is one of the oldest churches still in use in the United States.

Nemours Mansion is north of Wilmington. Alfred du Pont built this home in 1910. Art from around the world fills its 102 rooms.

Winterthur Museum and Gardens is northwest of Nemours Mansion. E. I. du Pont's daughter Evelina and her husband James Bidermann built this house in 1839. In 1951, the Bidermanns' great-nephew Henry du Pont turned the house into a museum. This 175-room museum contains about 89,000 furnishings from around the world. The furnishings date from 1640 to 1860.

Other New Castle County Sights

Newark is in western New Castle County. It is home to the University of Delaware. The university's sports teams are called the Fightin' Blue Hens. The blue hen chicken is Delaware's state bird.

The town of New Castle is east of Newark. It lies along the Delaware River. The Old

Court House is in New Castle. This building was the capitol for the Delaware colony from 1732 to 1777.

Delaware City is south of New Castle on the Delaware River. Pea Patch Island lies in the river east of Delaware City. The island received its name from a story that the colonists told. They said a boat carrying peas shipwrecked on a sandbar in the Delaware River. The peas sprouted and grew in the sand.

Legislative Hall in Dover is Delaware's capitol.

The colonists said the peas formed an island. Today, about 14,000 birds live on Pea Patch Island. They include ibis, herons, and egrets.

Visitors take ferries to Pea Patch Island to tour Fort Delaware. The fort was a prison for about 12,000 Confederate soldiers during the Civil War.

Kent County

Bombay Hook National Wildlife Refuge is in northeastern Kent County. This park covers nearly 16,000 acres (6,475 hectares) along Delaware Bay. Each fall, about 100,000 geese and ducks stop at Bombay Hook on their way south.

Dover is southwest of the refuge. Dover is Delaware's capital. Legislative Hall is the capitol building. Workers completed it in 1933. Visitors to Dover also can tour the State House. This building served as the state capitol from 1792 to 1930.

Dover Air Force Base is south of Dover. Large airplanes called C-5 Galaxies land there. These are the world's largest cargo airplanes. Visitors can see these airplanes and others at the Air Mobility Command Museum.

Sussex County

Sussex County is known for its beaches and historic towns. Lewes is near Delaware Bay. Today, visitors learn about the town's Dutch history at the Zwaanendael Museum.

The town of Rehoboth Beach is south of Lewes along the Atlantic Ocean. Since 1873, people have called this town "The Nation's Summer Capital." Many summer visitors come to Rehoboth Beach from Washington, D.C. They swim and sail. They also walk along the beach's 1-mile (2-kilometer) boardwalk. This wooden sidewalk is on the beach near the ocean.

Delaware Time Line

About 8000 B.C.—The first people arrive in what is now Delaware.

A.D. 1600—Lenape and Nanticoke people are living in what is now Delaware.

1609—English explorer Henry Hudson sails into what is now Delaware Bay.

1610—English explorers sail into what is now Delaware Bay. Captain Samuel Argall names the land and bay for Lord De La Warr, governor of Virginia.

1631—Dutch traders found Zwaanendael at what is now Lewes.

1638—Swedish colonists found the New Sweden colony and build Fort Christina in what is now Wilmington.

1655—The Dutch capture New Sweden and make it part of New Netherland.

1682—What is now Delaware becomes part of the Pennsylvania colony and is called the "Three Lower Counties on the Delaware."

1704—The Three Lower Counties break away from Pennsylvania and become the Delaware colony.

1787—Delaware approves the U.S. Constitution and becomes the first state to enter the Union.

1802—Éleuthère Irénée du Pont builds a gunpowder mill on Brandywine Creek near what is now Wilmington.

1829—The Chesapeake and Delaware Canal opens. The canal links Delaware Bay and Maryland's Chesapeake Bay.

1861–1865—Delaware stays in the United States during the Civil War.

1899—Delaware's legislature passes the General Incorporation Law. This law makes it easy to form corporations in Delaware.

1911–1924—Thomas Coleman du Pont builds the Du Pont Highway.

1933—Legislative Hall is completed and becomes Delaware's capitol building.

1971—Delaware's government passes the Coastal Zone Act.

1981—Delaware's government passes the Financial Center Development Act.

1987—Delaware celebrates its 200th birthday as a state.

Famous Delawareans

Valerie Bertinelli (1960–) Actress who starred in the TV series *One Day at a Time* and in many made-for-TV movies; born in Wilmington.

Emily Bissell (1861–1948) Activist who designed the first U.S. Christmas Seals to help people with tuberculosis (1907); born in Wilmington.

Annie Jump Cannon (1863–1941) Scientist who studied the stars; discovered more than 300 new stars and grouped stars by color; born in Dover.

Pierre S. "Pete" du Pont IV (1935–) Politician who served in the U.S. House of Representatives (1971–1977) and as Delaware's governor (1977–1985); born in Wilmington.

Henry Jay Heimlich (1920–) Doctor who developed the Heimlich Maneuver to save people from choking (1974); born in Wilmington.

William Julius "Judy" Johnson (1900–1989) Baseball player who played in the Negro Leagues

(1921–1938); later worked as a major league scout; named to the Baseball Hall of Fame (1975); grew up in Wilmington.

Ruth Ann Minner (1935–) Politician who served in the Delaware House of Representatives (1974–1982) and Senate (1982–1992); elected Delaware's first woman lieutenant governor (1992–); born in Milford.

Jay Saunders Redding (1906–1988) Author who wrote about being African American in books such as *On Being Negro in America*; born in Wilmington.

Judge Reinhold (1956–) Actor who starred in *Vice Versa* and in the *Beverly Hills Cop* movies; born in Wilmington.

George Thorogood (1951–) Rock musician who recorded many hit songs with his band, The Destroyers, including "Bad to the Bone" and "Move It on Over"; born in Wilmington.

Words to Know

broiler (BROI-lur)—a young chicken that is raised for its meat

chemical (KEM-uh-kuhl)—a substance used in or produced by chemistry; medicines, gunpowder, and food preservatives all are made from chemicals.

chemist (KEM-ist)—a scientist who studies or works with chemicals

Constitution (kon-stuh-TOO-shuhn)—the document that is the basic law of the United States

integrate (IN-tuh-grate)—to bring people of different races together in schools and other public places

peninsula (puh-NIN-suh-luh)—a piece of land attached to a larger land mass and surrounded by water on three sides

plantation (plan-TAY-shuhn)—a large farm where one main crop is grown

segregate (SEG-ruh-gate)—to keep people of different races apart in schools and other public places

textile (TEK-stuhl)—a fabric or cloth that has been woven or knitted

To Learn More

Aylesworth, Thomas G. and Virginia L. Aylesworth. *Mid-Atlantic: Delaware, Maryland, Pennsylvania*. Discovering America. New York: Chelsea House, 1996.

Brown, Dottie. *Delaware*. Hello U.S.A. Minneapolis: Lerner, 1994.

Fradin, Dennis Brindell and Judith Bloom Fradin. *Delaware*. From Sea to Shining Sea. Chicago: Children's Press, 1994.

Thompson, Kathleen. *Delaware*. Portrait of America. Austin, Texas: Raintree Steck-Vaughn, 1996.

Internet Sites

Excite Travel: Delaware, United States
http://www.city.net/countries/united_states/
  delaware

Hagley Museum and Library
http://www.hagley.lib.de.us

Historical Society of Delaware
http://www.hsd.org

Kalmar Nyckel
http://www.kalnyc.org

State of Delaware
http://www.state.de.us

Travel.org—Delaware
http://www.travel.org/delaware.html

Useful Addresses

Delaware Tourism Office
99 Kings Highway
P.O. Box 1401
Dover, DE 19903

Hagley Museum
P.O. Box 3630
Wilmington, DE 19807-0630

Historical Society of Delaware
505 Market Street
Wilmington, DE 19801

Kalmar Nyckel Foundation
1124 East Seventh Street
Wilmington, DE 19801

Nanticoke Indian Museum and Powwow
Routes 24 and 5
Millsboro, DE 19966

Index